Tuwyn

Poems
by
Kezia Sproat

Tuwyn -- Poems by Kezia Sproat
© 2019 by Kezia Sproat. All rights reserved.

Published by *Skye's The Limit Publishing & Public Relations, LLC*

This book may not be reproduced in whole or in part, in any form or by any means, electronic or mechanical, including photocopying, recording, or by any information storage and retrieval system now known or hereafter invented, without written permission from the publisher and/or author.

Books published by Skye's The Limit Publishing & Public Relations, LLC may be available at special discounts for bulk purchases in the United States by corporations, institutions, and other organizations. For more information, please contact the Marketing Department at Skye's The Limit Publishing & Public Relations, P.O. Box 133, Galena, Ohio 43021, (fax) 740-548-4929; or via e-mail at talk2stl@gmail.com

Book interior and cover design ©2019 by Skye's The Limit Publishing & Public Relations, LLC. All Rights Reserved.

The cover and interior art are based on "Great Blue Heron," by Jane Story Bost, collage artist, of Chillicothe, Ohio.

Skye's the Limit Publishing & Public Relations
PO Box 133, Galena, Ohio 43021
(ph) 740-913-1439
(fax) 740-548-4929
skyesthelimitpublishing.blogspot.com

Published in the United States of America, Ohio, Galena.

Hardcover:

    ISBN-13: 978-1-939044-42-6

Paperback:

    ISBN-13: 978-1-939044-41-9

Website: Tuwyn.blogspot.com

Library of Congress Control Number: 2018958825

PUBLISHER'S NOTE

Every possible effort has been made to ensure that the information contained in this book is accurate at the time of going to press, and the publisher and author cannot accept responsibility for any errors and omissions, however caused. No responsibility for loss or damage occasioned by any person acting, or refraining from action, as a result of the material in this publication can be accepted by the editor, the publisher, or the author.

Acknowledgements

The following poems, often in earlier versions, appeared in *Righting: Poems and Process*, ed. Margaret Honton (Columbus, Ohio: Argus Press, 1977): "Sexism," "OSU, The Oval at Noon," "Tuwyn," "Chicago Breakfast Poems," "The Great Depression of 1975," "Song," "Of an Ancestor Spearing Elephants Bogged in Swamps," and "For an Educator, Southern Ohio."

"Naming" appeared in *The Poet's Job: To Go Too Far,* ed. Margaret Honton (Columbus, Ohio: Sophia Books, 1985).

"Emotion," "The Next Time," "The First Position," "The Reformer," and "For My Daughters" appeared in *Re: Creative Writing*, ed. Margaret Honton (Columbus, Ohio: Sophia Books, 1985).

"The Destruction of the Little Art Theatre" appeared under a different title in *Poetry in the Park 1989* (Columbus, Ohio: Department of Parks and Recreation, 1990).

"A Child of the 50's Sings for Her Breakfast" appeared in *Women's Week Journal* (Columbus: The Ohio State University Women's Studies Program, 1975, vol 1, no 1).

Back cover portrait of Kezia Vanmeter [Sproat] by Clifford B. West. 1961, Kingswood School Cranbrook. For more information on the artist: *Oral history interview with Clifford West,* 1975 February 26-28. Archives of American Art, Smithsonian Institution. https://www.aaa.si.edu/collections/interviews/oral-history-interview-clifford-west-12100

Tuwyn

Foreword

I googled *Tuwyn*, thinking it must be an Old English hint of the book's theme. I was only half wrong. It is Kezia's toddler daughter's word for **turn**. And indeed, the poems suggest that life is a series of turns, a ballet on a numinous stage.

Youth/age, daughters/mothers, family/friends, ideal/real, city/country, love/loss, life/death: these seeming tensions are not opposed. Rather, "the edge curls and the surface swims." Only Bost's great blue herons do not turn but stand erect, patient and contemplative, elegant and autonomous, their beaks pointing the way to poems. Kezia the scholar enriches them with allusions to academia, literature, and film. Kezia the Chillicothean alludes to the people, flora, and fauna of Appalachian Ohio. These are mostly free verse poems, yet bits of rhyme, meter, and vestigial sonnets lurk in these pages where at times the everyday meshes with myth.

We meet prophets and martyrs, like the woman working in the A & P who "eats dime-a-loaf bread" in the spirit of "neglected plants" that "will kill themselves to keep their youngest buds alive." Alternately whimsical, humble, satirical, elegiac, the poet sings of the past, present, and future, of roads taken or not, of politics, social justice, anatomy, mortality, choices, and, supremely, of women's lives.

The imagery is lush: "fish who swim and look up at the sun," the figures striking: "a sea of thin green arms" for August corn, the poem "Shall We Go" simply breathtaking. West's drawing of the poet is the same Kezia Sproat whose class I wandered into when I was an inchoate eighteen-year-old, and that has made all the difference. I daresay she looks the same and still does her wonderful work.

Charlene Fix, poet
Columbus, Ohio

Charlene Fix is Emerita Professor, English, Columbus College of Art and Design. Fix received fellowships from the Ohio Arts Council and the Greater Columbus Arts Council, and has published poems in *Poetry, Literary Imagination, Hotel Amerika, The Manhattan Review* and others. Her most recent book is *Taking a Walk in My Animal Hat*. Earlier were *Flowering Bruno, Harpo Marx as Trickster*, and *Frankenstein's Flowers*. Fix received multiple awards from the Poetry Society of America. BS in English Education, Ohio State University, 1970; MA in English, Ohio State University, 1977.

Tuwyn

Contents

Acknowledgements i
Foreword. iii

1

Women of the World. 3
Song 5
Edges and Surfaces 7
Yoctangee Park, Chillicothe 9
Highbank, Appalachia 11
For an Educator, Southern Ohio 13
Tuwyn 15
The First Position 17
Open the Windows 19
Asthma in October 21
Naming 23
The Reformer. 25
Plato and Aristotle Meet for Lunch or, The Happy Nihilist 27

29

OSU, The Oval at Noon. 31
A Cold in January 33
Ads in *American Poetry Review* 35
The Destruction of the Little Art Theatre 37
Title Page for *The Letters of Shakespeare's Aunt Minnie* 39
A Valentine for My Dead Sister 41
A Child of the 50's Sings for Her Breakfast. 43
On Getting My PhD 45
The Great Depression of 1975 47
Dudley Hascall, in memory of 49
Sexism 51
Emotion 53

WPW Exercise Poem	55
Chicago Breakfast Poem: For Cornelia, 1974	57
Chicago Breakfast Poem: For Ellin, 1975	59
Chicago Breakfast Poem: Airport Conference 12/9/95	61
Chicago Breakfast Poem: Sequel 2009	63
Martin Luther King, Sr. at the Democratic National Convention, 1976	65

67

My Daughters, May 1983	69
Puberty Notice	71
Cornelia: The Artist as Model	73
Eliza, Madonna of the Animals	75
Cornelia, 1988	77
My Father, Chasing Foxes at Piketon	79
A Student of Physics, Highbank	81
My Mother	83
2B-16	83
Demand Not	85
Helen Rose Janes Vanmeter	85
To The Man Who Abandoned Our Children Ten Years Ago	87
Self-Portrait	89
Shall We Go?	91

Tuwyn

93

A Poem for the ERA, 1981 95
A Phone Call Tells of Sandy Johnson's Death 97
Morning Sisters (for Barbara)..99
Bill, I'm Sick of Writing Elegies (In memory of Bill Redding) 101
Cyce Tichener 103
Fran Wintner 103
John Charles Thomas Arthur Morrow..............................105
Oxford University Press 107
For A Very Sick Man..109
Stillborn..111
Howell 113
David libretto: Paltiel's Parting Song to Michal....................115
David libretto: Absalom to Amnon................................117
David libretto: Shimei's Curse at David 119
Romania, 1990: An Exiled Musician................................121
Comfort for Prufrock..121
Friends of the Homeless 123
Of an Ancestor Spearing Elephants Bogged in Swamps 125
Ubangis...127

Also by Kezia Sproat   128

Tuwyn

Tuwyn

**Poems
by
Kezia Sproat**

Skye's The Limit Publishing and Public Relations, LLC
Galena, Ohio
United States of America
©2019

Tuwyn

Securus judicat orbis terrarum,
bonos non esse
qui se dividunt ab orbe terrarum,
in quaecumque parte terrarum.

Tuwyn

Women of the World

Fetch water from the Garusaku
well, carry it twelve miles at dawn to
cut thirst to grind maize form a loaf

search

for a stick for fire
for something

to feed the children.

Paulette von Rabinov d'Este Soppofor,
Marchioness of Saintsbury,
considering the wedding ring she can no longer remove,
studies whether first to swim
or have her driver
take her to Antibes for lunch.

Tuwyn

Song

I am swimming.
I am a duck-billed platypus.
My child's name is Gringa.
Her cousin is Gringolet, Lochinvar's horse.
They play together often.
If you would like to join them,
Write them a letter: Tell them so.
Mail it to me. I will send it on.

They took me for a horse,
Put a bit in my mouth,
Pulled hard this way and that:
The corners bled; blood caked my face.
I was speechless.

Gringolet then bravely journeyed
over moors, under the seas,
came up on shore in New Jersey
galloped in mud to his knees,
knocked at a door by a marker:
putting great risk on his soul,
just to find out for Gringa
if this could be part of the Whole

Where starving and dying her children
cry in the city nearby, and
sheltered well, high in stone structures,
old men think they can tell why.
Devils served self-satisfaction
heaping on platters: they ate.

Gringolet galloped in horror
fled from their infamous feast
to Gringa the platypus baby
who looks for solutions at least.
Send your high thoughts out to Gringa
sisters and children of night.
Wrap them up, mail them out to me;
I will deliver to Gringa,
Gringa who sings in the sea.

Oceans waltz over high mountains
down by the depths in the sea.

Tuwyn

Edges and Surfaces

O All you souls who sleep beneath this rain
(Sister, rabbit, Son)
and All our souls who breathe in it above
struggle for the middle line between,
the edge, the surface of the soil.
This heavy August rain delineates unclearly
who is who.
We reach
below, and they reach up to drink.

So fish who swim and look up to the sun
and little boys who stare from banks above-
no fish or child can find a constant angle;

the edge curls and the surface swims.

To define oneself as dead or living, fish or person
Philistine, Greek, or Jew is pure presumption.

All is coming, and all is nearly gone.

Tuwyn

Yoctangee Park, Chillicothe

Mother once said your parents were so much in love
   with each other
they had no time for you, and I've always wondered
   how that would feel.
How would that be?

Some of the ducks in this park are domestic, some
   mallards becoming domesticates.
As we were, wild children, learning to be
proper on the outside, wild beneath,
alive.

This park is fine tonight. The grass races up the hill
to Water Street, its shops rowed up like Nantucket now.
The geese search under their wings, for bugs, I think,
or on the paths and in the grass
for picnics of their own describing.

From here, I can't see the tennis courts,
or hear the players chatting,
the thuds of balls on racquets.

Tuwyn

Highbank, Appalachia

Very little plastic is in this house
or anywhere around.
The barn is falling.
Robbers come at night.

Weeds rise up with the gravel drive.
For the axle, a huge hole waits, half-filled with concrete
by the rust iron plank-floor bridge,
forged, like the bricks, here.

West of the tenant house
is a porch,
Nothing
to sit on but boards,
for better thinking.

A muskrat house hunches up from the flood wash.
Five deer
cross the road behind us,
like dancers hired to make a film,
the cameras in our car,
watching.

Straw bales help
the joists and rafters bear the corn crib.
Only a hope of pigs and chickens keeps the little sheds alive.
This is heaven, and I am scared to stay alone.

Tuwyn

For an Educator, Southern Ohio

Between plowing time and first green growth
in fields around here, early spring,
arrow hunters walk the furrows, staring
carefully into churned-up ground,
hoping for roots and semblances
in small pieces of chipped stone.   Come see,
beneath this soil and in its wheat and bread
the ancient human past stays with us.
Molecules transformed--distant poets singing
now our shoes. We toil their presence.
Beside you now, their pale adopted children,
promising and withholding, mute as arrowheads,
spinning for transformation, Transformer,
tell them: Solomon yields to the lilies.

Tuwyn

Tuwyn

"Capital University Economics Professor
Predicts Death of City"

Today I went to the dying city.
Today I drove in the dying city,
in dying city's streets and alleys
where green laced between me and sky--
drove my Ford to the dying city,
took my child to the dying city--
lovely toddler, freckled, ringlets,
off the freeway, into alleys,
sailed in fast, then slowly turning,
"Tuwyn here," she said,
"I love to tell people where to tuwyn."

Near her father's house in the slums
a new garage door opened on an alley.
Tuwyning and leaving my delight in the ghetto
I went alone to the center,
through the center, past banks and towers and offices,
past a parking lot green at the fringes with shrubs
like a bald man with fuzz round his ears.

By a bank stood a black man
hosing the bushes half-hiding him.
Water arched up from his hose
as if he were a statue and fountain
smiling and fixed and
alive and calm in the morning.

Tonight I drove to the dying city
where I saw a herd of longhorn cattle
alive inside a plate glass building.
Here
tonight
my child
and I
will sleep.

Tuwyn

The First Position

The first position is either pain or joy.
Somewhere between the sunlight filtering
through the plane trees on
Leicester Square
and the bricks in the sidewalk beside
the British Museum
is a piece of orange air breathed
out once by Mohandas K. Gandhi --
lingering, poised, waiting
for the dirt that John Milton kicked off his boot
the night before he finished telling
Paradise Lost to his daughter,
which Granny heard; and you, my children,
listened when I told you about it.

Tuwyn

Open the Windows

For my students, harassed and angered

I forgot to tell you--I want you for another purpose.

When I left you and went to Babylon
(having finished my oration, my mouth full of dust)
I drove beside the river.
Rust-eaten rocker-panels were colliding,
cars filled with women and children,
crossing the waters
gaunt in the hopes of the north.
The woodsmen came from Kentucky
bearing on their backs aged brides, aging babies.

God bless the man who has everything,
for whom Tiffany's offers gold-engraved pet rocks
in the Sunday *New York Times*.
I forgot to tell you: I want you for another purpose.

God bless those transients by the waters
who wish their children, or some of them,
could stop at McDonald's, and
God bless those who have given up wishing.
God bless the Pope, old, sick, and cooped up in the Vatican.
I forgot to tell you: I want you for another purpose.

A shelf in the A & P holding Weight-Watcher's dog food
is toward the front, just behind the third register
where a jolly Appalachian woman works,
fat and getting fatter. She eats dime-a-loaf bread
instead of meat. Her children visit her at the store.
Neglected plants will kill themselves
to keep their youngest buds alive.

God bless my orthopedic surgeon who overcharges the
Welfare Department so much he has to make his patients
wait while he consults loudly with an investment
counselor about his oil well stocks.
God bless all orthopedic surgeons, eating broken bones,
and the welfare workers lunching out at Clyde's.
I forgot to tell you. I want you for another purpose.

Tuwyn

Asthma in October

I am a tree woman.
There is my head out there,
taller than my neighbors,
moving with the wind,
swaying. My hair
nonetheless stays arranged,
swaying gracefully with the wind.

Like a bather in the ocean,
floating in utter passivity
back and forth in the wind,
submerged in the wind,
of the wind, flying,
back and forth, around and
down and up and in no order
at all, no order at all, none.

Arms akimbo,
joints all jelly,
my branches could break
and I become all wind, all water, all flow,
a high Reynolds number.

But I am still free, not wind, not water;
the branches hold, leaves attached,
green in leaf-life,
holding on, resisting the
great and lovely force that is the wind,
but dancing with it.

Tuwyn

Naming

I heard what you said to Arlene, God,
the night they cut her leg off,
and what she said to you.
It gave me a new understanding of mathematics:
we all abide within one number, changeless,
no matter how the parts are divided.
How we talk, who we talk to, what we say
don't matter.

Realities differ: the nurses tell her,
because she's eighty-seven and may forget,
"You're in Riverside Hospital. This is 1983.
You've had surgery on your leg." But
as long as they're going to euphemize
cutting her leg off,
why not let her believe,
as her cries in the night indicate she does firmly,
that it's 1917 and she has the flu in Kansas.
Her mother's busy tending sister Jenny--
that's why she doesn't come.

Names shouldn't matter that much.
Adam named the animals to show he had power:
I was named John, renamed after birth for
a daughter of Job, whose pains made him
shakes fists like your servant Arlene,
whose lost leg is named by the nurses "surgery,"
but whose ears can't hear the comforting
Ghost whisper,

*Wherefore if thy hand or thy foot offend thee,
cut them off, and cast them from thee. It is better
for thee to enter life halt or maimed,
rather than having two hands or two feet
to be cast into everlasting fire.*

The nurses should dress up as Jesus and say that.

Tuwyn

The Reformer

I was born in crisp November,
instantly mounted my horse,
his black flank glistening,
the saddle ready, the stirrup fitting,
we galloped around the corral, inspecting.

For their good, we moved swiftly
stamping precisely at whatever
barbarians
dared stick their feet
through the fence boards.

Heedless of their grandeur
and obvious desires,
now I circle, circle
changing horses as necessary
when one and then another
fades or dies.

If horses fail me,
I write or lecture,
stamping, watching,
minding the fence rows
and even the shadows behind them:
my falcons light on any
whose energy, love of order, or righteousness
should flag.

The forest is careful:
trained constrictors patrol the quiet places.
Rarely does the world seep through the cracks.

A distant prophet told me
that one day this corral would open
and I would be led out
to see the shadows
and the figures between
these shadows and this fire.

What I will do then
is unclear,
or what I will say.

Tuwyn

Plato and Aristotle Meet for Lunch
or, The Happy Nihilist

The very best poem in all history is
unspoken, unwritten, unheard, unseen,
and will be forever.

The best way to communicate is just to
think about music:
don't write it down or make it up
as you go along--
it will be imperfect.
Don't play anyone else's on a machine--
the best source connected
to the largest number of
the best-placed, highest
quality amplifiers in the world
will not give you true sound.

But if you're having a bad day and
can't think about music adequately,
go to a concert--
somewhere, anywhere, the Ohio,
the Palace, Carnegie Hall, Sydney, Australia,
or down the street.

After the conductor has arrived
and the preliminary welcoming applause has died,
after the baton is raised,
there will be a moment when
everyone in the place
will be quiet.

Thousands will breathe as one, lightly,
before the music starts, a
moment, maybe two--

No matter how the concert is going to be,
that moment will be perfect.

(Cough.]

In real life, concerts start
with a bit of frivolity
for that very reason.

Tuwyn

OSU, The Oval at Noon

Step, step, steppity step,
quickly, briskly they go
off for lunch
at the Faculty Club,
walking all in a row:

in all weathers together,
as if in fear of being caught
peering out upon the land alone.
Always a leader and his pack,
the junior thieves march anxiously behind
until their backs are published.

Grass nor mud assail them not,
nor do they turn to see
waves exploding they walk through,
cry "Sister" or cry "Brother,"
nor raving youth, nor gorgeous age,
nor any of the many clear
mirrors of their fear.

Only hope of marching first in line some year
keeps them
trudging dolefully through the snow,
holding up the tail of a dead tradition.

Tuwyn

A Cold in January

Ladies and Gentlemen

Perked Bonnet Galleries
Is pleased to announce
That the complete works of Swami Microbius
Will be offered for sale
On Saturday, the 13th of February
At Murphy's Kitchen, one-hundred two
South Front Street.
As Everyone possessed
Both of Finesse and Gumption knows,
The great Swami works in
Vaporub and steamed-water design;
Hence, Murphy's Kitchen.

New Course Offered

The Department of Critical Analysis
Of the Sohio State University
Will offer an introductory course
In the works of Swami Microbius,
Spring quarter, 1976.
Professor Mucilage Gerbil, Chairman
Of the Department
Will trace the history of Vaporub and Steamed-Water Design,
Showing Microbius' unique contribution
To that tradition.
students will be asked to submit
Papers, either Charmin or Kleenex.

From the Faculty Blue Sheet

Professor Mucilage Gerbil's study,
"Some Thoughts on Vaporub"
Has been accepted for publication
By Kleenex Books.
Professor Gerbil's work was
Made possible
By a grant from the Charmin Foundation
Which provided funds for
A two-year investigation of the works
Of Swami Microbius, world's leading Vaporubist.

•••

Award Given

Little Billy Sunshine,
Assistant in the Department of Critical Analysis
At Sohio State University, has been awarded
The Distinguished Sycophant Prize
For his work with
Professor Mucilage Gerbil
On Vaporub.   Billy is the son
of Mr. & Mrs. Albert J. Fuchs
of 4023 Worminghamshire Drive West.
Billy read his paper, entitled
"A Few Thoughts on Vaporub"
At the fall meeting of the
Association for Critical Analysis
Held this year in Delhi, India.

Tuwyn

Ads in *American Poetry Review*

Promise lots of body language,
language bodies, murmurs, bodies clasping,
expanding thickly,
every teacher a name,
every name named, bandied, smiling, bodied.

Hear art oozing from well-defined souls,
feel actual loss and pain
(in case you've none of your own).

The huge block of ice from my dog's water dish
melts now in the kitchen sink.
It is complex and beautiful, carefully formed by
the Proud Ice People and the
Scurrying Aluminum People who made the old soup cooker
before it got its degree in being my dog's water dish, thus
    winning the honor of staying alive
    in another Republican administration.

Tuwyn

The Destruction of the Little Art Theatre

Tooth and claw contending, the mouth attached
giraffe-like, the machine's great neck
assures success, but for a moment
the marble cornice is itself possessed,
if not of life and living pilots,
of pride so great to say to all of us
assembled under floodlights--
"I am. I shall not come this way again,"
a sound so loud, passionate and
disinterested at once that in my
watching children's nervous laughter at the
hungry beast there is a promise
always to hear the marble cornice
voice in the heart's pavements.

Tuwyn

Title Page for *The Letters of Shakespeare's Aunt Minnie*

Being a collection of letters
found in a trunk beside a trash can
outside the back door of
the Pavilion of the Royal Opera, London,
by the Reverend Euthyphro P. McDougal on Nov 8, 1937;
Edited and rendered into 20th century English
by Kezia Bradford Vanmeter Sproat, PhD,
whose mother was a McDougal
on the left side.
Of interest to historians of the theatre
and family counselors alike.

Tuwyn

A Valentine for My Dead Sister

The women that we used to be
cramp down an overwhelming rage for life,
put curtains on our windows, all discretion,
pigtails dangling from our brains, our knees together,
white socks hold bare legs to tantalize
the school Principle's oldest boys,
who dream what's underneath our plaid starched dresses,
but do not read our writings, hear our songs.

We sound our words in daydreams,
change action into fantasy, survive
in most cases, move ever more slowly to the door
at the front of the house, fierce with hope,
press our faces on the window of the future,
cloud it with our breath.

Tuwyn

A Child of the 50's Sings for Her Breakfast

Ghost of Wallace Stevens,
tell me why,
stopping in McDonald's on my way to the OSU Library
at 9:00 on Tuesday morning
I got the same rush you described from the
oranges your heroine ate on Sunday in her peignoir?

She was comfortable and unharassed.
I'm unemployed, divorced, middle-aged, and fat:
what right have I to her complacencies--
that sense of calm and being-with-the-world,
what all these Jesus freaks would call, if it befell them,
grace?

McDonald's orange juice in a plastic cup, a foil lid?
The windows?
It may have been the windows, Wallace Stevens:
someone's washed them and they wrap around my chair
as if I were a captain of a ship
looking out on three sides to the sea.

Doing my own work of the mind,
being free to stop and write a poem,
having someone else make breakfast,
knowing guiltless I will walk out of here
any time I want to.   Wallace Stevens,

without you I might not have recognized the feeling,
nor made it so far as McDonald's.

But all my sisters, who
sit beside the dishes
crusty only with oatmeal for
moments before the baby cries
again or the washer (if they have one) needs
unloading . . . . . Wallace, male and a
banker, do you know what
they feel?

Tuwyn

On Getting My PhD

When I went out with the wheelbarrow
to make compost as a child--dump the family garbage
at the far corner of the yard, pitch clean hay on it--
the hired man's dog, who we thought ours,
ran large ferocious joyous circles
around me, crazed with joy at having company and dusk
and summer warmth--and maybe hope of sharing evening compost.
She died from eating chicken bones.
We mourned her like a brother.
She now lies still, and it is I who circle.
My muse, Adversity, is best on trouble,
straitening the tie-strings of my soul
to get them tight and see me run faster,
searching all the borders for the whole.

Tuwyn

The Great Depression of 1975

Mozart is for people with good jobs and clean houses-
those who can sustain order and bright melodies
without suddenly stopping to cry from time to time,
struggling to suppress an unexpected hysteria.

Beethoven is for the rest of us.

Whenever any Mozart comes unbeckoned,
surprising us from the radio,
whether we are aimlessly dusting the pedal assembly
under the piano,
or driving, charged with the most precious
of all human souls in heavy traffic,
we long with an inordinate passionate nostalgia

for pre-twentieth-century times,
before this latter traffic from the grave
that makes the very Twilight of the Gods
Arcadian; before electric men could sneer
and order over millions all at once;
before this latter fall, when
more of us could dance in our own meadows,

hearing Mozart.

Tuwyn

Dudley Hascall, in memory of

Fat Death leers his head over the horizon,
a humongous moon, jowls blowing, eyes bulging.
Before him run millions
in more or less expensive multicolored soft striped jogging clothes.
"Run, run from death," say the tall thin Battelle
executives with grey hair
to the short fat ones with blond hair, and they run
right on around King Avenue to the Santa Monica beaches.

Fat Death watches, still blowing and bulging, expressionless,
    having satisfied himself only this morning with
children from Brazilian favelas.

"Hi, Fat Death," I say, sitting in the middle,
watching the runners out of the corner of one eye
and His Holiness out of the side of the back of my head,
"Are you truly so fat and real?"
He doesn't reply, only keeps bulging, blowing, and scaring
people.

Curiosity pinions me
between the runners and the race;
but only a little shove,
a slightly stronger wind . . .

Tuwyn

Sexism

Lacoon, his sons
and the sea snakes
had nothing on my daughters and me.
They did not have to
breathe sea snakes,
but first had a
free life--
and after the attack,
a quick passing.

Tuwyn

Emotion

This gold chain around my neck
is the same one Chaucer says the world hung by
from heaven at the end of *Troilus and Criseyde*,
when Troilus looks down
at himself watching the Greek camp
in agony from the walls of Troy
and laughs. He is still laughing
at one end of my necklace.

Sometimes the chain becomes a gilded snake
and slides, slides watchfully around the town
opening its eyes at the town's mercies, closing and opening,
closing and opening its eyes on its shocks and its horrors,
unable to know if its tail is in Troy or in heaven.
Forgetting itself,
sometimes it slides to the OSU Library,
extends itself a hundred-fold,
twists and winds around the Utley fountain,
hugs it tightly, weeping.

Tuwyn

WPW Exercise Poem

Behind this mask is a face
looking through me
and through the hills behind me.

Between its eyes, gleaming like fish scales
are daffodils, nodding,
a brass mandala, and a giant pig.

Behind this mask is a face:
the all-knowing pig,
who makes no difference.

Tuwyn

Chicago Breakfast Poems

For Cornelia, 1974

I am overcome with a fierce desire
to be again in one of those fine hotels in Chicago
where the breakfast rooms murmur with quiet efficiency.
Waiters glide with trays of melons
to be placed on ice at the buffet.
Crisp women in shrimp-and-white starched cotton
respectfully request if you would like more coffee.

Once upon a time I read the day's program
of the Modern Language Association meeting
and decided first to hear a talk on Sartre, in French of course.
Around me, people from all walks of life--shopkeepers, scholars--
none infringed upon the mind of any other
in that quiet, bustling place, and all were paid for service.

This morning
I had to scrub the soaking spatula three times
to get off egg from yesterday.
I will stay, here, now,
and try to find some words to tell, someday,
the child who scrambles eggs and leaves the dirty
pan for me to scrub
is worth career, Chicago, all.

Tuwyn

Chicago Breakfast Poems

For Ellin, 1975

We found an early breakfast place
under the El:
grease-streaked table, plastic lions on the walls,
tired waitress.
At first we were the only ones
walking out to see the dawn,
resting here.

Suddenly the room filled up with men in work clothes---
one not to be forgotten, very tall and humble,
waiting patiently, sack lunch at his grey poplin-covered side,
wrinkled, early, tired, not sitting down for breakfast.
Awkward in height and poverty,
he might have been a Lincoln,
and ordered only coffee.

Chicago Breakfast Poems

Airport Conference 12/9/95

Dressed exclusively in concrete,
Where might be a mouse to eat
For the shivering hawk on the snow fence at O'Hare?
With grass so thin, is there any hiding?
Who controls his path amid the runways?
On the rapid transit, one of many voles,
I plunge through miles of treeless, grassless tenements,
aim to the Art Institute, for respite from
The Handgun Control Conference.
Run from the fear selling guns,
from ignorance, the sorrow of slums.
We may be voles for the shivering hawk,
Who knows?
I am the only one here from Ohio.

Tuwyn

Sequel 2009

Even then, the skinny kid
was here, figuring out
hawks and voles. Already had
his first date with Michelle
at the Art Institute.

Ever feel scared
or tremble at poverty?
or bitter
or even just sad?

Consider Chicago.
Ride the CTA. Look at pictures.
Organize.
Hope when it's hopeless.
Hope any way.
Hope all the time.

Tuwyn

Martin Luther King, Sr. at the Democratic National Convention, 1976

Before the singing began,
after the white southern widow in a
    fine pink dress said,
"Leave this hall--
go ouat on youah great mission,"

after his son's widow kissed the candidate,
the old man took his quiet
up and held it high for all to share--

astonishing the millions who remembered
the old singing
the old marching, the ancient agony,

"The Lord is in this place," said the old man.
In my atheist's heart
I believed it.

Tuwyn

My Daughters, May 1983

Poems of seashores, ride with me
to the forest and learn its secrets.
Prepare yourself for its anger.
I will nabble and crab at your heels,
coax and defend, embrace and embarrass you
with my old ways from old times and
friendlier, cleaner places.

Ferns bow before you, springs rise from your steps,
yet trillium, hart's tooth and thyme
cover the paths of the snake-slider,
the tromphing bear, the long-robed vulture,
and all those who hate themselves.

Wear thick boots: ride through it:
jump with your brother, the deer.
The snarling felt so loudly on the wind
will not catch, bind, choke and kill you
as it has your aunts, your many sisters.
You will be Britomart; you are Elizabeth--
queens of the jungle, lords of the city,
joyous at riding, courageous at night.

Tuwyn

Puberty Notice

Attention.   We were not
the people who carried
six quarts of popcorn
into University Flick II
in a Kroger sack
last August,
and rattled it during the quiet parts
of *La Strada*.

This was alleged.
We did have a fine time, though.
We are just 10 and almost 12,
and this is our first
really adult
film experience.

Tuwyn

Cornelia: The Artist as Model

Because it could change colors,
she fell in love with the sky
before anyone told her God lived there.

It does not watch her. She watches it.

When the day, like a swan singing,
throws its colors
wildly swinging
west and south,
she holds its angry joy,
keeping her breath all evening.

Tuwyn

Eliza, Madonna of the Animals

I'm the vine smothering the lilac bush.

"That's a terrible thing to say to an *independent* person,"
every syllable emphasized, loud enough for the other
people in the waiting room at the OSU Veterinary Hospital
to hear.

In her wide arms and lap lie two 11-year-old black cats,
    alive,
the female draped on top of her injured brother for comfort.

Four ancient eyes stare wisely from blankets,
neither more nor less ignorant and afraid
than the mother, and the daughter
who strokes the cat's head and smiles.

Tuwyn

Cornelia, 1988

"By the turn of the century American business had discovered
   Costa Rica."

Nothing in this world is too good for you.
Before you came back from Europe the last time
I took that big old walnut pepper grinder
I gave my father for Christmas in 1971,
the one Mother gave back when he died six months later,
And cleaned the bejesus out of it--

I got some Formby's and steel wool and rubbed all the gooey
disintegrated varnish off it, rubbed for
half an hour, one
big long brown pepper grinder,
One small part of your home.

I wanted it elegant. I wanted
you to be happy to be back,
to say,
"I *like* this place. This is a nice
place!" when you walked in,
and you did; I cleaned for two
months as you wandered.

Then within days, mourning the
distance of Greece, Rome, and Paris,
mourning the passing of some of your optimism
measuring the distance of most of your hopes,
You came to this evening, for many evenings
quiet, solemn, downcast,
locked yourself in the bathroom
after an inconclusive dinner.

"She's crying!" Your sister and
I go up, firm and calm at the
door, <u>Open the door, now</u>,
and we talk a long time, and I rock you like a
baby and we come back down and
eat some of the waiting chicken and I
finish the whole bottle of wine while you
recount your passage, and you watch about Costa Rica

While (in the kitchen) I clean grease and assorted
spots from the teapot and my Dad's pepper grinder.

Tuwyn

My Father, Chasing Foxes at Piketon

Here   we bottle time and August evenings.
        In the quiet distance, a fox will rustle a stick,
        You chase it, laughing across the cornfields,
            bumping the furrows
        ferociously in an old Cadillac phaeton,

        to show your delighted wife and bouncing children
        what it can do, what you can do.
        How curious you were – at 52, like a boy –
        to see the fox up closer, and have us see it.

        Now nearly 52 myself, chasing through cornfields again
        in a yellow Cadillac exactly 50 years newer than yours,
        only 70 miles north of my childhood and yours,
        I get my Cornelia her dinner:

        push up 315 to Easy Living, to the Kinnear Road computer center,
        wait two minutes in the evening sun
        (the pause in the score where the cellos don't play, only count)
        with a turkey and havarti sandwich
        for your tall, dark, unpretentious granddaughter –
        a bit sad at not having a father for a long time either.
        She sees us and smiles, the face of all the angels.

        Sailing cool and smooth at 40 miles per hour,
            in a sea of thin green arms,
            their tops above our heads –
        this August corn's scent calls the fox, recalls
        the flocking crows we followed summer evenings
        down hollows – Coon, Dead Man's, and Turkey Run – to their
            congregational roost:
        losing one in the winding roads and trees, waiting for another,
        and finding two or three flying toward a point,
        inviting ourselves to their haunts and secrets
        with no other purpose than to see
        their great dead roosting tree, and they on it.
        We glide back through the university fields to the highway
        (she'll be on time for her second job)
in
        the heart of
this
town.

Tuwyn

A Student of Physics, Highbank

For perfect straightness,
consider a flooded field in distant
moonlight.
Contrast the trees.
Turn out the car lights.
The staring deer jump north;
ducks still move south.

Look west, Eliza, where flashes of ponding
stretch deep in the harvested corn,
stopped only by the hills across the river,
where black-haired trees dance for the old green sky.

The bottoms road we nearly traveled,
daring the lonely night,
is absolutely
straight across the top with water.

Tuwyn

My Mother

0 bless thee, butter dish
the only purple crockery in the closet,
strangely shaped, unique among the dishes,
filled with water in the washer, nearly drowning,
you come back faithfully to serve,
a clean and royal spirit,
unchipped, independent,
necessary.

2B-16

2B-16 is the room off ICU
where you wait.
I've been here before.

I could be anyone.
This could be any room;
it happens to be 2B-16, Medical Center Hospital, Chillicothe.

Hamlet waited for Gertrude,
Telemachus for Penelope,
and I for Helen,
my mother
who could be anyone's mother,
any mother at all,
not even on this planet, but
anywhere.

The head nurse said,
"Wait here.
It will be at least 20 minutes."

Tuwyn

Demand Not

Crushed between two stones, the generations
of Mother and daughters, I slide along the floor
licking up crumbs and dirt, and coming to a pile of crap
I toil in desperate thought: ultimate questions boil down,
to eat or not to eat it. Submerge, demand not, that you
may be the more demanded of, o pancake self.
forget to cry, so you can be a vegetable
sooner than your neighbor who goes
by the usual route, through the grave and up again.

Helen Rose Janes Vanmeter

God will not let us die till we are wise,
until we see how grass forms riverbanks
how the alligator rests in his chase of the horse,
how canelands broke for the buffalo,
and how they are breaking now.

Sooner or later, we will be wise
and shining,
our hands and our voices one,
feet unscathed by sorrow,
heart of the heavens, light.

Tuwyn

To The Man Who Abandoned Our Children Ten Years Ago

I worry when the dog barks at night
who it is.
This dog doesn't know you:
if you came back to see your daughters,
you might come to the same house,
see the same bushes, only larger,
the darker color of paint,
the new fence that keeps this large animal off some of the
backyard grass--
in general, the same comfortable level of disrepair--
even the same old cat you knew as a kitten,
waiting for you as Odysseus' dog waited for him,
on the brink of death all the time now.
You might wonder if it would be all right to knock,
if the dog would forgive you too.

Tuwyn

Self-Portrait

By day I do business;
at evening, a scholar; and
in the night a poet,
creeping like a rat among the dustballs of the mind,
sniffing for odorless pearls . . .

What's this?   Here is one!
Tomorrow it shall be peddled brazenly in the marketplace
as a thing of great value.

My heartbreaking children have left for the
evening in questionable company.

There may be a real mouse in this room--or it
   could be the furnace--

the Edgar Poe of late 20th century women,
totally shameless, at last.

Tuwyn

Shall We Go?

To Beijing? Taipei? Alexandria?
Swimming?   Crazy?
Beloved of all the world.

Dancing above the Olentangy Village pool
in the geranium trees of the spirit,
that boy's soul waited,
hovering, for two, then three hours
two years ago on your birthday.

Last night I walked in the corner
of the pool where he drowned.
For me, he's down there
in a wet suit, a weight belt, flippers,
holding his breath too long,
practicing for scuba.

Also, I pray, always hovering above
    (as intent as the terrified,
    hopeful motionless white women
    who circled his departure),
his spirit and life-love protecting
your travel, your body, your spirit,
from the long-gone horse-riding Mongols
and the small unseen enemies--hate, fear, despair.

Tuwyn

A Poem for the ERA, 1981

You--young woman who cried
in the alley beside my house this morning,
you sounded like one of my daughters.
Your chokes chilled my heart.

You were a block away
by the time I connected you to those cries.
You kept walking, straight, so
I did not embarrass you by shouting,
"Are you all right? May I help?"

Why did you cry
this balmy October morning?
Some man, no doubt.
Did you find him with another lover?
Did it break your heart?

Take comfort: amuse yourself
with the cats on this porch,
the dogs in this yard:
they will requite the slightest affection.

Take comfort: inside sits one
who cried on countless mornings in the alleys
and now laughs.

Or did you fight with your mother?
Take comfort: inside sits one
who has forgiven five hundred mothers,
and been forgiven a thousand
times by daughters like yourself.

Keep walking, straightforward.
We need each other.

Tuwyn

A Phone Call Tells of Sandy Johnson's Death

Have your phone disconnected, John Manning.
Clean it off with alcohol. Wrap it up in plastic.
Tell the phone company to trace its life and
cauterize all past connections.
cut the wires now--what delivers that message
must never work again.
It's not you, John, it's the phone--
I will not stand machines that lie.
It is they, not we, who die.
We must all get machete knives
and practice, and wield them
against yours and all telephones,
and cut all the lines and wires that lie to us.
We must get machete-wielders
on every block of every town in Ohio,
and the movement must grow and
killing telephones must become
accepted practice around the world.

It would be no use.
We would tell these things some other way,
our voices instantly ugly, unwelcome.
Had there never been telephones, and people
could not speak across distance by machine,
they would find some other way.

Sandy would speak and has spoken
by painting the lie on death,
brushing away mortality, sorrow,
translating spirit to long-lived leaves for jungles,
to feathers for peacocks.
A flying squirrel played a violin in a tree;
the butterfly danced intense and delicate
on the rhinoceros' horn:
we first heard a drum, then a flute,
then the world's whole natural orchestra.
The raccoon said, "Art is life."

Tuwyn

Morning Sisters
(for Barbara)

These spring days are for mourning sisters.

Instead,
we celebrate

          by being first at the artist's garage sale,
          hurrying out to buy vegetables,
          planning a trip to England.
          We will take our children.

          Yes, we eat LIFE for breakfast,
          filling our mouths with both bare hands.
          weeding our gardens, mowing, pruning, planting.

          That's how to do it:

these
          spring days are for morning,
sisters.

Cornelia Vanmeter Metzger
8/21/35-5/6/71

Sandy Hill Johnson
6/14/41-4/22/78

Tuwyn

Bill, I'm Sick of Writing Elegies
(In memory of Bill Redding)

Cutting deep to the real poem
during your funeral, I found myself
six hundred miles away, looking at ugly pictures
by Georges Braque and Pablo Picasso, and
seeing, hearing, touching, and smelling
three Puccini operas,
(a sad story of dock workers, a pregnant nun).

In an effort speaking of public relations as well as art,
the diva allowed management
to announce to the whole house
she'd lately suffered food poisoning--
a cheap way to excuse the possibility
of a less-than-perfect performance.

She brought down the house as the dead and dying nun.
   (I ate a sandwich of undetermined contents during second
   intermission.)
Should the understudy have been given a chance?
The diva more discreet about vomiting and diarrhea?
   (The tray had been sitting there for hours,
   the waiter's accent told me in subtext, "Eat it or faint.")

Or
Was it correct, best, and proper,
to make the honest announcement?

You would know that, and five million other points
in
a
moment,
Always laughing at any inherent dubiety,
so we would know without feeling stupid,
how much to take seriously,
without your having to tell us.

It's OK, you said:
"We write elegies to re-invent the dead.
Because we love these people
and the world
and want to share them."

Tuwyn

Cyce Tichener

Transfixed,
I could not see you.
But I know you were the one who pulled me up
dispelled the fear
gave me comfort
quietly,
as if nothing had happened.

Fran Wintner

The last time you came to my house
You treated me like a child,
"Sit down.   Stop fussing."
You were already relaxed, the greatest honor.

With every muscle I emulate your aspect,
your behavior: confident, skilled, controlled,
wide-visioned, sympathetic--but not too.

The assurance of the queens of ancient Greece,
watching above the fray and suffering in it
at once.

My mother does not come here.
This house is yours to command.

Tuwyn

John Charles Thomas Arthur Morrow

In the end, as in the beginning,
it all comes down to black and white--
we join the dark silhouettes on the horizon in
The Seventh Seal,
remembering their influence on the last dance in
8 1/2
the arms high bearing out Hamlet's body,
and all that followed that production.

A thin little boy with a long name
who haunted the Cleveland theaters.
We sat at your feet
drinking the lore you gave us
drinking the cosmos through thrust round proscenium
filters.

Watching you do the ironing was more interesting than
reading Shakespeare,
reading your footnotes, than watching the Sadler's
Wells Ballet.

Tuwyn

Oxford University Press

Neither epidermis nor ego,
brick nor stone,

can erase

the loss of my edition of the *Upanishads*
with a blue, black, and white
broad-striped cover,
that I bought at Vassar in the fifties
and must have lent to a friend in the sixties
or a student in the seventies
and can't find now anywhere
for anything.

Its voice is a child's,
but my child does not know it;
my brain hoard, like Caliban's,
grieves for lost music,
submerged in the sea.

Tuwyn

For A Very Sick Man

Here on a grassy bank
I try to relax,
to find a way between the leaves
out to the open air or water,
and breathe, gills or not.

You're out there, I read, in the water
gloating along;

An arm rises, brandishes time
like Excalibur.

Tuwyn

Stillborn

Watching you wake up
somewhere between yellow and green
bloated from the IV,

suddenly saying "I'm so happy
I don't have cancer."   Not knowing
how to respond, I say "I am too." No matter
how much care I take,
a certainty of inadequacy
assails me; words,
always my friends, fail.

Like rocks that fall off mountains in avalanches,
the child died,
escaping the twentieth century.

You want others fervently,
rejoice in a uterus, ovaries.

A gorgeous hope cleans contempt
from the world, propells
your lifeless son
to the arms of God.

Tuwyn

Howell

Great spirit, every night since your body
was cremated,
unable to sleep,
I have made popcorn.

If you have a skillet large enough, and a proper
lid for it, not too heavy, not too light,
the corn will hit the lid and sing
as a steel band sings,
in a scale and measure unknown to Mozart or Brahms.

Now who will call us with plans, the more impossible the better?
Who will wring delight from improbabilities and dust?
or kindness from cruelty?

And who can open the ears of the unvarnished truth?
Everyone you knew
was
without exception
perfect.

In 1976, Howell Price, a composer, music historian, and close friend, asked Kezia to write the libretto for *David*, a "musical mystery play" he envisioned, based on the Biblical accounts of the life of King David. The form Price conceived blended modern opera and medieval religious teaching dramas called "mystery plays." It was planned for production in an Episcopal Church in New York City. The work was never finished; Price died in 1978. The following three poems are from the *David* libretto.

Tuwyn

David, A Twentieth Century Mystery Play

Paltiel's Parting Song to Michal
Act II, Scene 2

I will take you to the wide place in the river
To the wide place in the river of my mind.

I will stay there and I'll love you there forever
At the wide place in the river of my mind.

Many other kinds of rivers flow around us
All their power and their glory surely try
to keep us from believing in each other
But you'll stay here in the river of my mind.

Tuwyn

David, A Twentieth Century Mystery Play

Absalom to Amnon
Act II, Scene 5

Stand back from that abyss.
Reptiles have a series of eyelids.
If the greed ever thins, dries,
scales and falls from your eyes,
your remorse will be desperate and thorough.

A many-lidded lizard will change to a man.
You will again cry out, prompted by
some private pain,
see God, and beg forgiveness
from people who were your
sisters in another life.

Tuwyn

David, A Twentieth Century Mystery Play

Shimei's Curse at David
Act II Entr'acte

So you are crossing the river
leaving the city in fright
I rejoice, I delight, O King in your anguish.

The sands on the bottom of Jordan will not outnumber your sins
The sands in the river are your brothers,
So pointless, so low is your life.

Your righteousness is a cloak –
Old and torn now, as I delight to see it –
A robe, to be lifted or worn as it suits, when you need it.
When you intend parading in the streets,
Your search through your closets
"Ah ha!" you say –
"This will make me look righteous – this I will wear today."

King, in Thebes of Egypt are a hundred gates
and through each gate a thousand horsemen pass:
The hairs on the tails of the horses of Thebes
are fewer in number than your crimes,
and all their droppings together
do not stink like your hypocrisy.

My ancestors join your children to curse you,
as you go whining across Jordan.

You sit with your friends on pillows
and leave there the smell of camels.
The palace reeks of your odor
Your servants even creep away for air.

Swine will forecast eclipses before you find understanding;
Before you win insight, before you have holiness
Water will flow up mountains and crows will sing like larks.

{David orders his troops not to retaliate.}

Tuwyn

Romania, 1990: An Exiled Musician

Hope comes dripping from the bathtub
 in a clean flowing robe,
comfortably rapt:

His hair still wet from washing the blood out,
his eyes still glassy from the long fever,
his feet connected to the clean earth,
for the first time he can ever remember.

Comfort for Prufrock

Looking from eyes outside ourselves
stiff with hairspray, cautious in high heels,
we held up mirrors and found
fearful captured birds.

Wounds healed, re-opened, healed again
from beating the sides of our cages,
we have developed immunities
the privileged cannot imagine.

Tossing what we don't need and
reaching for what we do,

We may be calling you. How will you know? Who are we?
Alfred, dear, I'm not surprised you had to ask:

We are serving tea, we are charwomen, mermaids,
swimming and scrubbing and serving

all together now, all together now.

You can relax too, honey.
Mama will take care of you.

Tuwyn

Friends of the Homeless

Four hundred years ago in London,
a poet was unheard of.
No one knew him or where he lived.
Family troubles had sent him to the city.
His kids back in West Virginia hungry,
one dead, his proud old father in disgrace.

Maybe he held horses by a stage door.
Maybe he lived nowhere . . .
Maybe he lived here.
934 East Main Street, Columbus.

Tuwyn

Of an Ancestor Spearing Elephants Bogged in Swamps

I hear you crying, cousin Matthew, on the beach
and wonder if you also saw him there
beyond the Straits of Dover in Androna,
attack our monster-brother in the swamp,
dig out his brains and eat them,
raw.

Retreating into parlors stuffed with plush
and bored, we tinkered with our toys all
painted green and splotchy, learned to fly,
did great restraint in Viet Nam,
to learn today, on best authority
(Joseph C. Harsh in *The Christian Science Monitor*),
they play our games again in other places, other skins.

And what a piece of work is man, my gentle cousin,
and what a piece of work has woman left to do
for pity for the mother elephant
for pity for our sister nursing cow
straining to push her calf from swamp and fire:
pity's work is what is left, my cousin:
pity's work is what is left to do.

Tuwyn

Ubangis

When we were little we twisted
our long hair up,
stuck pencils through the top knots,
and called ourselves Ubangis.

Next we went to the best schools to
analyze Keats and Shakespeare
and marry boys who decided about
which bank to sell and when to buy and when
the time was right

to bomb Cambodia.
No one we knew lived under that much foliage.

Those who married deciders
quickly wilted.

Long ago in soft bright confidence
we believed ourselves
more civilized than the Ubangis.

Now, we know who we are.

Securus judicat orbis terrarum,
bonos non esse qui se dividunt
ab orbe terrarum
in quaecumque parte terrarum.

Also by Kezia Sproat

- "A Reappraisal of Shakespeare's View of Women." Columbus, OH: dissertation, Ohio State University, 1975.

- "Re-reading *Othello*, II, 1." *The Kenyon Review*, 7(3), 44-51. 1985.

- *A Short Course in Nonviolence*. Chillicothe, OH: Highbank Farm Peace Education Center, 2001.

- [Editor] *In Tune with the River, A Part of the Bridge,* Collected Poems of Ellin Carter. Columbus, OH: Women's Poetry Workshop, 2007.

- A second book of poems, *Eh Ti Zwell,* is expected early 2019.

Tuwyn

www.ingramcontent.com/pod-product-compliance
Lightning Source LLC
Chambersburg PA
CBHW060459240426
43661CB00006B/856